INCREDIBLE QUOTATIONS

230 Thought-Provoking Quotes With Prompts to Spark Students' Writing, Thinking, and Discussion

by Jacqueline Sweeney

New York ○ Toronto ○ London ○ Auckland ○ Sydney

DEDICATION

*For Padre Tom Cassidy (el viejo), Arya Maloney, and Anandi Friend,
in the order of their appearance in my life—at the precise moments
I most needed the kindness of their presence and philosophies.*

ACKNOWLEDGMENTS

A special thank-you to Liza Charlesworth, who openly received and encouraged the concept for this book and editorially guided it to its public destination; and to Terry Cooper, whose presence is always felt behind each Scholastic Professional Book.

Thanks also to the graciousness of the principals, teachers, librarians, and reading specialists of the following Upstate New York schools: New Paltz Middle School and Elementary School (Lenape); Germantown Elementary; Scotchtown Avenue School (Goshen); Elm Drive Elementary (Millbrook); Gardnertown Fundamental Magnet School (Newburgh); Gayhead (Wappinger's Falls); and Red Mill, D. P. Sutherland, Green Meadow, and Belltop (East Greenbush).

To Sadie Friedman and Joanne Ferdman for captively listening to endless litanies of quotes, and to Norma Sweeney and Bettie Berge for accurate input on family history for the introduction.

A final thanks to my agent, Marian Reiner, whose energy inspires as she adroitly continues to tie up all those loose ends I'd never even recognize, much less tie!

Cover design by Jaime Lucero and Vincent Ceci
Interior design by Jaime Lucero and Liza Charlesworth for Grafica, Inc.
ISBN 0-590-96378-3
Copyright © 1997 by Jacqueline Sweeney.
All rights reserved.
Printed in the U.S.A.

TABLE OF CONTENTS

When I was a child, we'd often visit my Aunt Doris, who lived in a Civil War farmhouse in West Virginia. On cold winter mornings, my cousins and I would jump under the quilt on my Aunt's big bed and listen to stories about our ancestors. Over and over we'd hear about family characters: Uncle Emer, who ate everything with a sharp knife (even peas!); Aunt Jean, who died of pneumonia at age four, and who supposedly still visited the place of her birth. We'd imagine her haunting the bedroom in Virginia where our mothers were born and our grandmother had died.

The charcoal portrait of "the man in black" hanging over granddad's fireplace in Virginia, turned out to be our great grandfather, whose artistry is on display in the Smithsonian, and earned him the nickname "Potter John." Many times we were paraded past our great grandfather's pottery in the museum. But nothing impressed us as much as the story of his escaping discovery by the soldiers during the Civil War by walking backwards in his own footprints and hiding in a hollow tree.

Susan B. Anthony

All at once Potter John became real. As children, we might not conceive of ourselves as artists, but we sure could have hidden in that tree! Back then I might not have imagined myself a writer, but I could still hear the footsteps of those soldiers crunching snow in the dark.

These stories of family history were the beginning of my lifelong interest in biography. I was curious about the early lives of people I admired, and constantly searched for something *more* than historic rhetoric and museum portraits could offer. By the end of fourth grade I had read every biography in my school library (some two or three times). Constantly searching for role models, I burned to know what my hero (or heroine) of the hour was like as a child: Was she good in school? Did he play a musical instrument? Did he hate certain foods, tease his sister? Was there a hint of future greatness in her early life? I wanted to get to know the real Ben Franklin, Susan B. Anthony, and Lou Gehrig.

If Tecumseh could walk away from the tribe bully as a child, so that his example might promote peace, so could I. If Eleanor Roosevelt agonized over moral dilemmas, such as whether or not to turn in a friend for cheating in school, then her future achievements also deserved my scrutiny. And if one or more of my biographical examples kept a journal where she shared noble thoughts and dreams of better times, so could I.

I borrowed philosophies of life and survival from everyone. Ben Franklin was the first to encourage me to "smile in the face of adversity," while Jack London taught me how to stay alive in temperatures below fifty degrees. Rachel Carson warned me to cherish the five A.M. symphonies of songbirds (instead of having no birds at all to growl at for waking me up!), and Thomas Aquinas (nicknamed "The Dumb Ox" in school for his slow learning style) convinced me I really wasn't "stupid" in math when I couldn't fathom initial concepts as quickly as my classmates.

After a blitz week of reading the biographies of the Mayo Brothers, Sacajawea, Will Rogers, Wilma Rudolf, and Babe Ruth, I felt there was nothing I couldn't achieve if I set my mind to it. By God, if Hannibal could hoist those elephants over the Alps, and Sojourner Truth could risk death to get her young son back from slavery, and Potter John could dig clay from Dry River to make a work of art—so could I.

Of course I hope *Incredible Quotations* prompts discussion, and laughter and ethical thinking in your classroom, but it would be especially nice if it prompted a few "So could I's." I think that's the real reason I wrote it.

USING THE QUOTATIONS IN YOUR CLASSROOM

The quotations and prompts in this book may be used in a variety of ways in your classroom: as a beginning and/or ending to the day; in connection with social studies, language arts, and science curricula and themes; and as springboards to writing and debating activities.

Some of the quotations may contain words which are unfamiliar to students. Because of the nature of quotations, the context often may not offer enough clues for students to determine the meanings of the new words. You may wish to provide definitions when you present the quotation or have a dictionary available for students to consult.

Brief biographies accompany some of the quotes. You may wish to supply additional biographical material or have students research the lives of any/or all of the speakers.

A QUOTATION A DAY

What better way to begin the day than with a quotation? Before students arrive in your classroom, write a quote on the chalk board, After you or a volunteer has read the quotation aloud, use the prompt to discuss it. This beginning activity can help focus students' attention and strengthen critical-thinking and verbal skills. Consider ending the day with a quotation as well. In this case, you may want to have students write their responses in journals. Involve students individually, or in small groups, in selecting and presenting the daily quotations.

Will Rogers

THE CURRICULUM CONNECTION

The quotations in this book will enrich your curricula and themes. Hearing and reading the words of real people can personalize the study of social studies, language arts, and science for students.

Several chapters have strong social studies connections—"African-American Voices," "History Lessons," "Women Past and Present," "Who's in Charge?" "Lending a Helping Hand," and "Wisdom Around the World."

Many writers—representing different genres and time periods—express themselves in these pages. Use the chapters "Writers' Words" and "Book Talk" with your language arts curriculum. Consult the index, too, for the names of writers you want students to study. Encourage them to begin reading lists of authors and books, and evaluate the lists for appropriateness of material, reading levels, and interest.

"Our Place on Planet Earth" offers a thematic tie-in to science. For instance, What better way to open your students' eyes to the world around them than by quoting John Muir when he said: "The clearest way into the universe is through a forest wilderness."

PROVOKING THOUGHT

The quotations by themselves are thought provoking, and the prompts are designed to heat up the thinking process. Feel free to modify and add to the prompts. As students become more comfortable with the format, they may come up with their own questions.

Present quotations at journal time. Read the prompts, and have students record their thoughts. They may also want to begin collecting quotations and creating their own books. Some students may enjoy making a "quotable calendar" by assigning a quotation to each day. Other students may create quotation trading cards, which include quotations and biographical information.

Debating the pros and cons of the quotations will strengthen students' verbal and debating skills. Begin by letting students argue for the side about which they feel the most passionate. As they gain more confidence in presenting their thinking, arbitrarily assign them to either pros or cons. Students who remain uncomfortable about speaking may present their arguments in written form.

As John F. Kennedy said, "Too often we enjoy the comfort of opinion without the discomfort of thought." Using these quotations and prompts in your classroom may help your students enjoy and appreciate the "comfort of thought."

John F. Kennedy

I AM SOMEBODY

1

"To be nobody but yourself—in a world which is doing its best, night and day, to make you everybody else—means to fight the hardest battle any human being can fight, and never stop fighting."

— ee cummings
(American poet and playwright)

Describe yourself. Now describe yourself as you think others see you. How do the two descriptions compare? What is the hardest battle you've had to fight?

2

"No one can make you feel inferior without your consent."

— Eleanor Roosevelt
(Former First Lady, reformer, and humanitarian)

Eleanor Roosevelt

Think of an instance when someone tried to put you down. What did you do? If you're satisfied with the way you handled the situation, tell why. If you're not, explain what you would do differently.

3

"If I am not for myself, who will be?"

— Pirke Avoth
(Wise sayings of rabbis who lived in the 2nd century)

What's one thing you'd like to do more than anything in the world? Convince yourself that you can do it. What problems does this raise? How can you solve them?

4

"If you have no confidence in self you are twice defeated in the race of life. With confidence, you have won even before you have started."

— Marcus Garvey
(Political activist)

Marcus Garvey organized the United Universal Negro Improvement Association, the first mass movement among African Americans, in the 1920s. He had little support. Why do you think that confidence is so important in helping someone reach a goal?

John F. Kennedy

5

"Once you say you're going to settle for second, that's what happens in life, I find."

— John F. Kennedy
(35th President of the United States)

What philosophy of life does Kennedy share with Garvey (page 7)? Think carefully about each man's idea, and then respond to the following with your own ideas:

1. *Share a personal goal that you're determined to achieve.*
2. *Now share a goal you'd like to achieve—but you aren't sure you can.*
3. *What makes the first goal different from the second goal?*

6

"The significance of a man is not what he attains but rather in what he hopes to attain."

— Kahlil Gibran
(Lebanese poet, philosopher, and artist)

What do you think Gibran means? Do you agree? Tell why or why not?

7

"You have to expect things of yourself before you can do them."

— Michael Jordan
(Professional basketball player)

Think of a time when you asked more of yourself than you thought you could do. What was the result?

Mini-Bio: Michael Jordan
(Born: February 17, 1963)

As a child in Brooklyn, New York, Michael Jordan never even considered becoming a basketball player. In high school he was 5 feet 10 and sat on the bench a lot because the coach always chose taller players. "I made up my mind right then and there," said Michael, "that this would never happen to me again." He worked extremely hard on his basketball skills, and he also grew 5 more inches—to 6 foot 3—the summer before his junior year. In college, Jordan played for the North Carolina Tarheels. As a freshman, his winning shots at a tournament made him a hero. After participating in the 1984 Olympics, Michael Jordan turned professional and became the National Basketball Association (NBA) Rookie of the Year. He won the NBA's scoring title, most valuable player award, defensive player award, and is a superstar for the Chicago Bulls. All this from a kid who started out "short" and didn't even want to play!

8

"If you don't have confidence, you'll always find a way not to win."

— Carl Lewis
   (Olympic track star, winner of nine gold medals)

What do you think Carl Lewis means by this statement? Give an example of someone you know (it could even be yourself!) who talked himself or herself out of winning because of self-doubt.

9

"Every man has his peculiar ambition."

— Abraham Lincoln
   (16th President of the United States)

Abe Lincoln's "peculiar ambition" led him to be a lawyer and eventually President of the United States. Not many people believed he'd achieve either goal. Share your own "peculiar ambition"—no matter how far-fetched it sounds. Remember Abe!

Abraham Lincoln

10

"If, at the end, I have lost every friend on earth, I shall have one friend left and that friend shall be down inside me."

— Abraham Lincoln

Have you or anyone you know ever lost a friend because of your convictions and beliefs? Explain what happened.

11

"What saves a man is to take a step. Then another step. It is always the same step, but you have to take it."

— Antoine de Saint-Exupéry
   (French author of *The Little Prince*)

What difference does it make if a person keeps taking steps or just stops? Create two scenarios: one about someone who keeps moving, and another about someone who remains in one place. What does taking one step at a time teach you about achieving any goal?

12

"We are all worms, but I do believe that I am a glow-worm."

— Winston Churchill
   (Prime Minister of England 1940-45, 1951-55)

Choose an insect, fish, or animal that suits you. Complete the sentence below, and then explain why you chose that particular creature.

We are all _____, but I do believe that I am a _____.

13

"I've always been obsessed with logical thinking. I used to argue with my teachers when things didn't make sense to me."

> — Joanna Cole
> (Author of *The Magic School Bus* series)

If you're like Joanna Cole, you can't stop thinking about logical thinking. Have you ever argued with a grownup when something didn't make sense to you? Outline the argument and both points of view.

Joanna Cole

14

"If I could press a button and in the next fifteen minutes see the pyramids and be back home again, I'd do it."

> — Phyllis Reynolds Naylor
> (Author of *Shiloh*)

If you could press a button and in the next fifteen minutes see anything in the world, what would you choose? Give the reasons for your choice.

15

"One of my earliest recollections is of my mother singing. She sang from one end of the day to the other."

> — Ashley Bryan
> (Author and illustrator of *Lion and the Ostrich Chicks and Other African Folk Tales*)

Can you recall an early memory that affects your thinking or influences something you like to do today? Share your memory and its effects.

16

"You don't have to fight dragons to write books. You just have to live deeply the life you've been given."

> — Katherine Paterson
> (Author of *Bridge to Terabithia*)

"I think of writing as a way of seeing. It's a way of bringing out the special-ness of ordinary things."

> — Laurence Yep
> (Author of *Dragonwings*)

Who is your favorite author? How has this author helped you live your life more deeply and/or look at things differently? It may be the way the writer describes something, or how she or he makes you feel what the characters in the story are feeling. Describe one way this author has changed your way of living or seeing.

17

"My favorite book as a kid was *The Little Engine That Could*. I still go, 'I think I can, I think I can,' when I'm feeling insecure."

— **Paula Danziger**
(Author of *The Cat Ate My Gymsuit*)

What special words do you say to yourself when you're feeling scared or insecure? Where did your special words come from? If you don't have any, make up some words that you think would make a person feel better when he or she is feeling sad, or frustrated, or insecure.

18

"Everyone lives by selling something."

— **Robert Louis Stevenson**
(Author of *Treasure Island*)

Although Robert Louis Stevenson became a lawyer, he never practiced law. He preferred to write. Do you think the quote reflects Stevenson's experiences as a writer or his experiences as a lawyer? Explain whether or not you agree with him, and include an example of something you would or wouldn't sell.

19

"I hated toast. So instead of eating it, I would hide it. The closet in my bedroom was stacked with toast."

— **James Marshall**
(Author of *Miss Nelson Is Missing*)

Do you have any habits like James Marshall's—or do you know anyone who does? Describe one habit. What do you think is behind this habit?

Mark Twain

20

"The difference between the right word and the almost right word is the difference between lightning and the lightning bug."

— **Mark Twain**
(American author and humorist)

What do you think Mark Twain is saying about the process of writing? Have you ever felt this way when you were rewriting your own work?

21

"Good fences make good neighbors."

— Robert Frost

What do you think Frost meant? If you were building a house, would you put a fence up between you and your neighbors? Why or why not?

22

"Going to school after living on a farm was a very frightening experience. I learned to be very quiet and to observe. I had to learn how I was supposed to act."

— Beverly Cleary
(Author of *Ramona the Brave* and *Dear Mr. Henshaw*)

Describe a situation or experience where you didn't know how to act. Think about your first day of school, for example, or a first visit to a new place. What observations that you made on that first day or visit helped you later?

23

"The wastebasket is a writer's best friend."

— Isaac Bashevis Singer
(Polish-American author who wrote in Yiddish)

Do you agree that cutting out words, or editing, is the most important part of writing? How do you feel about cutting out parts of what you've written—even when you know it will improve the work?

24

"To have great poets there must be great audiences too."

— Walt Whitman
(American poet)

What kind of audience for poetry are you: great, terrible, or somewhere in between? How do you think Walt Whitman's words might apply to other art forms besides poetry such as, music, painting, sculpture, or dance?

Mini-Bio:
Walt Whitman

(Born: May 31, 1819;
Died: March 27, 1892)

Walt Whitman is considered the first great male American poet, and he walked a lot of roads to get there. For one thing, Whitman educated himself through reading and talking to people individually as he went on long walking tours of the West, South, Southwest, and Canada. Whitman's most famous volume of poetry is *Leaves of Grass*, which started out in 1855 as a 95-page book and grew to 456 pages by 1860. This book was the first of its kind to glorify the common people, and the "ordinary" way of life. Whitman thought poetry should sound like the speech of the people from which it came, and his poetry did. It sounded like America and Americans and reflected all the different jobs Walt himself held as a carpenter, typesetter, doctor's and lawyer's assistant, teacher, newspaper reporter, editor, contractor, real estate salesman, Army nurse, and federal government employee.

25

"Each human is uniquely different. Like snowflakes, the human pattern is never cast twice."

— Alice Childress
(American actress and playwright)

What if we weren't like snowflakes? What if every human being was exactly the same? How would our lives change?

26

"Your children need your presence more than your presents."

— Jesse Jackson
(Civil rights activist)

What do you think Jesse Jackson meant by this statement? Do you agree with him? Why or why not?

Shirley Chisholm

27

"It really takes guts to take a stand."

— Shirley Chisholm
(First African-American woman elected to U.S. Congress; first woman to run for President)

Have you ever taken a stand for something you believe in, even though your opinion was not a popular one? What led you to take this stand?

28

"We will have to repent in this generation not merely for the vitriolic words and actions of the bad people, but for the appalling silence of the good people."

— Martin Luther King, Jr.
(Civil rights activist and youngest winner of the Nobel Peace Prize)

Based on the quote, what do you think the word "vitriolic" means? Look in the dictionary to check your definition. Give two examples of vitriolic actions. Balance the words and actions of bad people against the silence of good people. Which side do you believe does more harm?

Mini-Bio:
Mary McLeod Bethune

(Born: July 10, 1875;
Died: May 18, 1955)

As a child, Mary McLeod Bethune saw her hardworking father cheated out of money because he couldn't read. This impressed her so much that when she was told that, as a black child, she was not allowed to learn to read, something inside her exploded. By the age of seven, Bethune not only knew how to read but was teaching others. The pursuit of her dreams led her to found and become president of Bethune-Cookman College in Daytona Beach, Florida. As a pioneer in the education of black children, she also rallied people in the fight for equal rights. Four presidents recognized Mary McLeod Bethune as a woman born to lead and appointed her to many government posts. She became the first African-American woman to head a federal agency, the Division of Negro Affairs of the National Youth Administration.

29

"Love builds…"

— Mary McLeod Bethune
(Founder and president of
Bethune-Cookman College)

What kind of "building" do you think Mary McLeod Bethune is talking about? What has love built for you? Do you think there is anything more powerful than love? Explain your answer.

30

"The life of the nation is secure only while the nation is honest, truthful, and virtuous."

— Frederick Douglass
(Orator, abolitionist, and former enslaved person)

Frederick Douglass, who said these words in the 1840s, opposed slavery and fought for civil rights long before the civil war. If you could do two things to help keep your nation "honest, truthful, and virtuous," what would you choose to do? (Hint: You might wish to change an already existing condition.)

31

"There was never a time in my youth, no matter how dark and discouraging the days might be, when one resolve did not continuously remain with me, and that was a determination to secure an education at any cost."

— Booker T. Washington
(Educator and author)

"Look inside to find out where you're going, and it's better to do it before you get out of high school."

— Artist formerly known as "Prince"
(Composer and musician)

Both the artist formerly known as "Prince" and Booker T. Washington are talking about education and life goals. What are your life goals? (Think for a moment about what you might want to do to support yourself and/or a family some day). How do you think an education might help you achieve these goals?

Bill Cosby

32

"I don't know the key to success, but the key to failure is trying to please everybody."

— Bill Cosby
    (Actor, comedian, and Doctor of Education)

Have you ever had an experience where you tried to please everyone and no one was happy; for example, making a family supper or planning an outing with friends? If you could relive this experience, what would you do differently?

33

"When the sun is shining I can do anything; no mountain is too high, no trouble too difficult to overcome."

— Wilma Rudolph
    (Olympic track star)

What makes the sun shine for you? How do you feel when it's shining? List the things it makes you want to do.

34

"Friends are my heart and my ears."

— Michael Jordan
    (Professional basketball player)

What are friends to you? Make up your own definition of friends.

35

"Don't be in a hurry to condemn because he doesn't do what you do or think as you think or as fast. There was a time when you didn't know what you know today."

— Malcolm X
    (Former leader of the Nation of Islam; founder of Organization of Afro-American Unity)

Do you ever find yourself becoming impatient with someone younger than yourself? Why do you think this happens? Do you recall anyone older who was impatient with you? How did that make you feel?

Malcolm X

Mini-Bio:
Sojourner Truth
(Born: 1797; Died: 1883)

The word "sojourner" means traveler, and that's exactly what Sojourner Truth did for almost 20 years, criss-crossing the United States to speak out against slavery and for women's rights. Born into slavery in Hurley, New York, she was originally given the name of Isabella Baumfree. Separated from her son by the institution of slavery, Sojourner Truth won a lawsuit against an Alabama slave owner and had her five-year-old son returned to her. After the Civil War, she became the first "Freedom Fighter" by helping newly freed slaves adjust to freedom. Slavery was outlawed in 1863 when Sojourner Truth was 68 years old. Until her death, she worked to keep it that way.

36

"I'm a self-made woman."

— Sojourner Truth
(Formerly enslaved woman and advocate for emancipation and women's rights)

Sojourner Truth made this statement in the late 1800s. What do you think she meant? Suppose a 20th-century woman made the same claim. What do you think she would mean?

37

"If you learn to THINK BIG, nothing on earth will keep you from being successful."

— Benjamin Carson
(Surgeon)

Name at least one way you THINK BIG in your life. Do you know anyone who THINKS BIGGER than you do? Tell what the differences are between your thoughts.

38

"We don't ask a flower to give us any special reasons for its existence. We look at it and we are able to accept it as being something different, and different from ourselves."

— Gwendolyn Brooks
(Pulitzer Prize winning poet; poet laureate of Illinois)

Substitute the word "person" for "flower." What deeper issue do you think Gwendolyn Brooks is talking about?

HISTORY LESSONS

39

"A people without history is like wind on the buffalo grass."

— Sioux proverb

What do you think this proverb is saying? Explain why you agree or disagree with it.

40

"No army can withstand the strength of an idea whose time has come.

— Victor Hugo
(French author of *Les Misérables*)

The French Revolution started with an idea whose time had come, and so did the American Revolution and the civil rights movement. Think of other major events in history that began with an idea whose time had come.

41

"We must honor our ancestors."

— Alex Haley
(Author of *Roots*)

What do you do to honor your ancestors? How would you like to be honored by future generations of your family?

42

"The memories of men are too frail a thread to hang history from."

— John Still
(16th century English writer)

Have you ever heard the expression that history is constantly being rewritten? Why do you think this happens? Is it a good idea to have more than one historian writing about the same event? Explain your answer.

Henry Ford

43

"History is more or less bunk."

— Henry Ford
(American inventor)

Do you take Henry Ford's side, or do you think he's full of bunk? Present an argument to back up your opinion.

Woodrow Wilson

44

"A man's rootage is more important than his leafage."

— Woodrow Wilson
(28th President of the United States)

"The child is father to the man."

— William Wordsworth
(19th century English poet)

What do these two quotes have in common? What do you think each man is saying about personal history (our families and how we're raised)?

Name two qualities—likes or dislikes and habits—you have now that you think you'll probably still have as an adult.

45

"As there were no black Founding Fathers, there were no Founding Mothers—a great pity on both counts."

— Shirley Chisholm
(First African-American woman elected to U. S. Congress; first woman to run for President)

Do you think the history of our country would be different if women and African-Americans had been included in its founding? Give an example of how their participation in the past might have affected our lives today.

46

"Those who cannot remember the past are condemned to repeat it."

— George Santayana
(American philosopher)

Which important historical happening would you want your children to remember, so they will never let it happen again? Think about wars, slavery, the Holocaust, and so on. Be specific when you answer this question—remember, there have been many wars, and many instances of slavery and discrimination all over the world.

47

"What you really value is what you miss, not what you have."

— Jorge Luis Borges
(Argentinean poet and critic)

Suppose this is a lesson in your personal history. Think of someone who is no longer here—a teacher, scout leader, coach—whom you miss? What do you value most about your memory of this person? If this person were standing in front of you, what would you say to him or her?

48

"When it is dark enough, you can see the stars."

— Charles A. Beard
(American historian)

Difficult (or "dark") times often bring out the greatness in people. With this in mind, what do you think Beard is saying? Name someone in history whose greatness has emerged in a time of turmoil.

49

"Learning is not attained by chance, it must be sought for with ardor and attended to with diligence."

— Abigail Adams
(Former First Lady)

Can you think of something you've learned, either at home or in school, that took a lot of patience and hard work on your part? How did you feel after achieving your goal?

50

"That's one small step for man, one giant leap for mankind."

— Neil Armstrong
(U. S. Astronaut and moon walker)

What do you think Neil Armstrong is saying about each person's role in history? Do you think history can be made by just one person working alone? Explain your answer.

51

"We are not makers of history. We are made by history."

— Martin Luther King, Jr.
(Civil rights activist)

Name one way you feel you've been "made" or formed by history? Consider your attitude towards others, the way you think about life, education, the freedoms you have that you didn't have to fight for and so on.

Mini-Bio:
Martin Luther King, Jr.

(Born: January 15, 1929; Died: April 4, 1968)

On the bus ride home after winning a prize for his speech about the Constitution, Martin Luther King, Jr., and his teacher Sarah Bradley were taunted and humiliated because they refused to give up their seats to white passengers. King felt betrayed that the Constitution didn't protect people of his race (as his prizewinning speech said it did). "That night will never leave my mind. It was the angriest I have ever been in my life," he wrote later. Rather than lash out, King turned his anger into a mission encouraging nonviolence. He devoted his life to the organization of people working to achieve peace and equality for all races. Using Mohandas Gandhi's model for nonviolent resistance, King never lost his dream of full civil rights for all. He was awarded the Nobel Prize for Peace in 1964, the youngest person to receive the award.

Rosa Parks

52

"I believe we are here on planet earth to live, grow up, and do what we can to make this world a better place for all people to enjoy freedom."

— Rosa Parks
   ("Mother" of the civil rights movement)

Why do you believe we were put on planet earth? What do you think you might do to make this world a better place?

53

"Nature never did betray the heart that loved her."

— William Wordsworth
   (19th-century English poet)

What does this quote say about the relationship between humans and nature? Present an incident that shows nature's betrayal. What role, if any, did human actions have in that betrayal?

54

"...Anger at the hunters...who slaughter everything that creeps or walks or flies...at myself...the young man who thoughtlessly committed the same crimes against nature."

— Scott O'Dell
   (Author of *The Island of Blue Dolphins*)

What do you consider to be "crimes against nature"—hunting animals, oil spills in the ocean, clear cutting forests, or other acts? Tell how you first became aware of the problem.

55

"Flowers...seem to smile, some have a sad expression, some are pensive...others again are plain, honest and upright."

— Henry Ward Beecher
   (American clergyman)

Choose two (or more!) of your favorite flowers. Describe them in terms of having human feelings and expressions. A pansy, for example, might look like a quiet old woman while a sunflower might look like a giant, yellow rock star. Study pictures in books or magazines, and let your mind go!

56

"No one in the world needs a mink coat but a mink."

— Anonymous

Defend or argue against this statement. There have been cases of people throwing paint on expensive coats made of animal fur. They want: 1) to show their anger at the killing of animals; 2) to ruin the pleasure of wearing these coats. What do you think about these tactics?

57

"California is a nice place to live—if you happen to be an orange."

— Fred Allen
(American humorist)

Using your knowledge of habitats, fill in the blanks below. For instance, you might match the words "swamp" and "alligator" or "tundra" and "snowflake."

_____ is a nice place to live—if you happen to be a(an) _____.

58

"The most important thing about Spaceship Earth—an instruction book didn't come with it."

— Buckminster Fuller
(designer who created the geodesic dome)

You've been asked to write an instruction book for the earth. What are your first three instructions?

59

"The clearest way into the Universe is through a forest wilderness."

— John Muir
(Father of the National Parks)

What do you think John Muir means by "clearest" in this statement? Describe the most peaceful experience you've ever had with nature (it might be a camping trip, walking in the snow, or daydreaming from the top of your favorite tree, etc.). Be sure to include how this experience made you feel.

60

"The bluebird carries the sky on his back."

— Henry David Thoreau
(American philosopher and poet)

What does your favorite bird carry on its back or wings or beak? Before you decide, think of its color, shape, how fast or slow it flies, and so on. Look up the bird in an encyclopedia, too, and then complete the sentence below.

The _____ carries (the) _____ on its back.

61

"April is the cruelest month."

— T. S. Elliot
(American poet)

Which month do you consider the cruelest? Which month do you consider the kindest? Explain your reasons.

62

"Women can do everything; men can do the rest."

— Russian proverb

Do you think this proverb was written by a man or a woman? Give the reasons for your opinion.

63

"Some of us are timid. We think we have something to lose so we don't try for that next hill."

— Maya Angelou
(African-American poet)

Have you ever sat on the sidelines rather than try something new such as playing a sport or singing in front of others, because of shyness or the fear of looking foolish? If you could live that moment over again, how would you change it?

Maya Angelou

Mini-Bio:
Hillary Rodham Clinton
(Born: October 26, 1947)

As a child in Chicago, Illinois, Hillary Rodham once had to contend with a bully. On the advice of her mother, she stood up for herself and fought back. Hillary Rodham also gained valuable lessons from being a Girl Scout and playing competitive sports. At the age of 14, she even wrote to NASA about becoming an astronaut. At Yale Law School, Hillary Rodham's chief interest was the legal rights of children. She also discovered politics there—and Bill Clinton, who became her husband. As First Lady, Hillary Rodham Clinton continues to focus her energy on helping children and improving health care and education. She considers her family "... the most important thing in my life."

64

"You win one day, you lose the next day, you don't take it personally. You get up every day and go on."

— Hillary Rodham Clinton
(First lady, lawyer, and advocate for children's rights)

What do you think about Hillary Clinton's point of view? Have you ever felt like pulling up the covers and not getting out of bed because you were disappointed about something? What made you get out of bed?

65

"You can't change the world. You can only change yourself."

— Beatrice Wood
(American artist)

Beatrice Wood was 102 years old when she gave the above advice! If you could change one thing about yourself today, what would it be? If you could change one thing about the world today, what would it be?

66

"We hold these truths to be self-evident, that all men and women are created equal."

— Elizabeth Cady Stanton
(Women's Rights Activist)

Elizabeth Cady Stanton, a friend of Susan B. Anthony's, fought for women's rights in the 1800s. Back then, most people did not agree with the above statement. Do you know anyone today who would not agree with this statement? If this person were standing in front of you right now, what would you say to him or her?

67

"Never doubt that a small group of committed citizens can change the world. Indeed it is the only thing that ever has."

— Margaret Mead
(American anthropologist)

You and a small group of people intend to change the world. What will be your first step? What will you do next?

68

"I know I'll survive. I'm a fighter."

— Shirley Chisholm
(First African-American woman elected to U.S. Congress; first woman to run for President)

When you fight for something, does it always have to be with fists? Describe a way you can fight without violence.

69

"Many persons have a wrong idea of what constitutes true happiness. It is not attained through self-gratification but through fidelity to a worthy purpose."

— Helen Keller
(Author and advocate for the deaf and blind)

Blind and deaf since infancy, Helen Keller never waivered in her quest to help others. Do you think she was a happy woman? Explain your answer.

Helen Keller

Harriet Tubman

72

"Woman must not depend upon the protection of man, but must be taught to protect herself."

— Susan B. Anthony
(Women's Rights Activist)

Do you agree with Susan B. Anthony? Why or why not? Do you think it's a good idea for women to learn some form of self defense? Are there other ways to protect oneself besides learning judo or karate?

Susan B. Anthony

70

"… there was one of two things I had a right to, liberty or death. If I could not have one I would have the other…I should fight for my liberty as long as my strength lasted."

— Harriet Tubman
(African-American nurse, spy, scout, and conductor on the Underground Railway)

What two things do you think you have a right to? What would you be willing to do to keep these rights? Explain your answer.

71

"When you decide to give yourself to a great cause, you must arrive at the point where no sacrifice is too great."

— Coretta Scott King
(Advocate for peace and racial equality)

Think carefully, and then choose a cause for which you'd consider no sacrifice too great. Consider politics, marriage, the environment, world peace, and so on.

73

"Look at me! Look at my arm! I have plowed and planted, and gathered into barns, and no man could head me—and ain't I a woman?

— Sojourner Truth
   (Formerly enslaved woman and advocate for emancipation and women's rights)

Think about some of the activities that you've accomplished in your life. Share your list with other students. Can you label the activities as "female" or "male"? Do you disagree about some of the labels?

74

"Most people think I am a dreamer…. We need visions for longer things, for the unfolding and reviewing of worthwhile things."

— Mary McLeod Bethune
   (Founder of Bethune-Cookman College)

What are your visions for the future? Share one of them.

75

"I shall persevere in spite of everything, and find my own way through it all, and swallow my tears."

— Anne Frank
   (Jewish teenager who died in a Nazi concentration camp during World War II)

One of the ways Anne Frank persevered was by recording her secret dreams and thoughts in a diary. What do you do when you feel alone and need comforting? What other ways can you think of to get through tough times?

Mini-Bio:
Anne Frank
(Born: June 12, 1929; Died: 1945)

Anne was born in Germany during a time of great turmoil. Many people had no jobs. Many more were listening to the frenzied speeches of Adolph Hitler, who fed anti-Jewish feelings. When Hitler became Chancellor of Germany and began to actively persecute Jews, Anne and her family were hidden by Dutch friends for four years. During this time, Anne kept a diary, in which she shared her feelings about her fear of being discovered. She also shared her belief in the goodness of people, despite the horrible happenings of the war that surrounded her. After being discovered and transported to a concentration camp in Germany, she died there. She was 15 years old. Her writings have inspired millions and keep alive the memory of those who died in the Holocaust.

76

"The man with the real sense of humor is the man who can put himself in the spectator's place and laugh at his own misfortunes."

— Bert Williams
(Vaudeville comedian)

Do you believe that laughing at yourself can make a bad situation better? Recall a time in your life when you felt frustrated. Would laughter have made you feel better?

77

"Comedy is simply a funny way of being serious."

— Peter Ustinov
(English actor and author)

Think about a favorite funny movie or television show that also had a serious theme. How did the movie or show use humor to get its message across?

78

"Wit has truth in it, wise-cracking is simply calisthenics with words."

— Dorothy Parker
(American writer)

What do you think Dorothy Parker means by this statement? Is there anything good about wisecracking? Can you think of an example of wit "that has truth in it"?

Mini-Bio: Will Rogers
(Born: November 4, 1879; Died: August 15, 1935)

Will Rogers was a late bloomer. As a boy he was shy and did poorly in school. His parents were one-quarter Cherokee, and Will attended a one-room Cherokee school in Oklahoma, where he was born. Continuing his education at the Kemper Military School in Missouri, Rogers spent his time roping, clowning, and playing tricks. Later he became known as the "Cowboy Philosopher" and is still considered one of the greatest ropers of all time. He also gave lectures, starred in movies, wrote a Sunday column for *The New York Times* and other papers. He never lost his integrity or his good will. As Rogers said, "I joked about every prominent man of my time, but I never met a man I didn't like."

79

"Everything is funny as long as it is happening to somebody else."

— Will Rogers
(American humorist)

Put yourself in the following situations: a) a bus drives through a puddle, splashing water all over you; everyone around starts laughing, and b) you see someone get splashed by the bus and start laughing. Describe your reactions to laughter in both situations.

80

**"If called by a panther
Don't anther."**

— **Ogden Nash
(American humorist)**

Make up your own funny saying. Play with language like Ogden Nash does, for example: Don't wait for a turtle, she won't hurtle.

81

"Once you get people laughing, they're listening and you can tell them almost anything."

— **Herb Gardner
(American playwright, whose specialty is comedy)**

How is Mr. Gardner's advice valuable? Have you or anyone you know ever used humor or comedy to get people's attention (in life or in writing)? Was that use of humor successful, or did it backfire? Explain.

82

"Laughter is the shortest distance between two people."

— **Victor Borge
(Comedian and pianist)**

Analyze Victor Borge's statement, and restate it in your own words. Have you ever been in a friendship that began with laughter? Describe your first meeting with your friend.

83

"I don't deserve this award, but I have arthritis and I don't deserve that either."

— **Jack Benny
(American comedian)**

What would you say to someone who truly deserved a compliment or an award, but said he or she didn't deserve it? How would you deal with someone who does the reverse, and continually asks for compliments yet doesn't deserve them?

84

"I'm a deeply superficial person."

— **Andy Warhol
(American artist)**

Many of Andy Warhol's paintings depicted celebrities and every day things such as soup cans. For this reason, he wasn't considered a serious artist by some people. Based on Warhol's quotation, do you think he cared what people thought?

85

"The reports of my death are greatly exaggerated."

— **Mark Twain
(American author and humorist)**

This is how Mark Twain responded when he read his obituary, or announcement of his death, in the newspaper. How does this humorous statement make you stop and think? Does knowing the statement is based on truth make it funnier?

86

"People who live in glass houses shouldn't walk around in their underwear."

— Bill Cosby
(Actor, comedian, and Doctor of Education)

Bill Cosby took a cliché and made a new saying out of it. Create a new and humorous saying out of one of the following clichés: a) The early bird catches the worm, or b) It's no use crying over spilled milk.

Mini-Bio:
Bill Cosby
(Born: July 12, 1937)

Bill Cosby grew up in Philadelphia during the years of the Great Depression. Fifty years later, in 1987, he was the highest paid entertainer in America. Still, Cosby prefers the honor "Most Popular Entertainer" for his work on "The Cosby Show" because it means he was appreciated by ordinary people. At the age of 35, he returned to school to get a doctorate in education, partly because he never felt complete after leaving college to enter show business. When Cosby returned to television, he was Dr. Cosby. He even employed a Harvard University psychiatrist as a consultant for "The Cosby Show" to be sure family values were accurately portrayed.

87

"I'm not afraid to die. I just don't want to be there when it happens."

— Woody Allen
(American writer, movie director, and comedian)

What situation would you like to avoid? Come up with your own quote about it. How can humor help lessen our fears about certain situations?

88

"You must lose a fly to catch a trout."

— George Herbert
(English poet)

Write a humorous imitation of George Herbert's quote, for example: You must lose your hat to catch a cold. Consider other things you can catch such as baseballs or footballs, animals, trains or buses, and so on.

89

"When you've got an elephant by the hind leg, and he is trying to run away, it is best to let him run."

— Abraham Lincoln
(16th President of the United States)

Have you ever taken on a task that seemed to be as big and difficult to handle as an elephant? What was the outcome? How would Lincoln's advice have helped you with your task?

90

"Never give in, never give in, never, never, never—in nothing great or small, large or petty—never give in except to convictions of honor and good sense."

— Winston Churchill
(Prime Minister of England
1940-45, 1951-55)

Do you agree or disagree with Winston Churchill? Cite an example from your own life to support your view.

91

"A president's hardest task is not to do what's right, but to know what's right."

— Lyndon B. Johnson
(36th President of the United
States)

What do you think Lyndon Johnson meant by this? Do you believe a president or leader can always do what's right? Explain your answer.

92

"No government ought to be without censors; and where the press is free, no one ever will."

— Thomas Jefferson
(3rd President of the United
States)

In some countries, people give up their lives for criticising their governments' policies or officials. How do you imagine America might be different if we didn't have freedom of the press?

93

"Associate with men of good quality, if you esteem your own reputation; for it is better to be alone than in bad company."

— George Washington
(General, 1st President of the
United States)

Do you agree with George Washington? Did you ever know someone whose behavior changed for the worse because of the "company" he or she was keeping? Why do you think this person is so influenced by others?

George Washington

94

"I suppose leadership at one time meant muscles; but today it means getting along with people."

— Indira Gandhi
   (First woman Prime Minister of India)

Define your idea of a leader. Put yourself in the position of someone who leads and then of someone who is being led. Does the change in roles change your definition of a leader, and if so, how?

95

My people are few. They resemble the scattering trees of a storm-swept plain..."

— Chief Seattle
   (Native-American leader)

Since a leader is a person who is responsible for the welfare of others, how do you think Chief Seattle must have felt when he said this? Have you ever been responsible for the welfare of someone or something besides yourself (perhaps as a babysitter, or being in charge of a pet).

96

"Nothing is more difficult, and therefore more precious, than to be able to decide."

— Napoleon Bonaparte
   (Emperor of France)

What's the most difficult decision you ever had to make? What made it so difficult?

Mini-Bio:
Abraham Lincoln
(Born: February 2, 1809; Died: April 15, 1685)

Because he always had to work (plowing, planting, feeding animals, harvesting crops, chopping trees, and splitting rails), Abe Lincoln always told people he went to school by "littles." And though his total schooling at ages 11, 13, and 15 didn't add up to one year, Lincoln read every book he could borrow. Some he copied, so he could read them over and over. Every night Lincoln read by candlelight (a favorite was a biography of George Washington). At 21, he left home with nothing but his clothes. His many jobs included postmaster of New Salem, Illinois (at age 24); surveyor; and mailman. Hungry to learn, Lincoln taught himself what he needed to know to become a lawyer. He was known far and wide for his honesty and his sense of humor, which made him a popular candidate for the legislature. Our 16th President, Lincoln suffered with everyone in the nation during the Civil War. His greatest hope was to keep the North and South together and "bind the nation's wounds."

97

"No man is good enough to govern another man without that other's consent."

— Abraham Lincoln
   (16th President of the United States)

When Lincoln said these words over a hundred

years ago, the United States was divided, primarily over the issue of racial equality. Do you think the issue of racial equality has truly been settled? Tell how you arrived at your answer.

98

"We are not interested in the possibilities of defeat."

— Queen Victoria
(Former Queen of England)

Can you think of any other great leaders who felt this way? How might you apply this philosphy to your own life (consider challenges in school, sports, with friends, etc.)?

99

"Great events make me quiet and calm, it is only trifles that irritate my nerves."

— Queen Victoria

Have you ever witnessed a crisis (an accident, a weather or medical emergency)? Did you notice how some people were calm and some fell apart? Why do you think Queen Victoria's attitude is probably a good one for someone in a position of power?

100

"If you are as happy, my dear sir, on entering this house as I am in leaving it and returning home, you are the happiest man in the country."

— James Buchanan
(15th President of the United States)

"I feel like the man who was tarred and feathered and ridden out of town on a rail."

— Abraham Lincoln

James Buchanan made his remark as he was ending his presidential term and leaving the White House. To whom was he speaking? Abraham Lincoln! The quote from Lincoln expresses his own feelings about being President.

After reading the remarks of Buchanan and Lincoln, do you think you'd like to have the position of President? Why or why not? If you were President, what's the first thing you'd do?

101

"There is nothing wrong with America that cannot be cured by what is right with America."

— William J. Clinton
(42nd President of the United States)

Do you agree with this statement? Name two things you think are right with America, and two things you think are wrong with America. If you had the power to correct the wrong things, how would you do it?

Franklin D. Roosevelt

102

"We have nothing to fear but fear itself."

— Franklin D. Roosevelt
(32nd President of the United States)

Can you think of a time in your life when your fear of something frightened you more than the thing itself? For instance, have you dreaded a trip to the dentist that turned out to be fine? Have you worried about a quiz you aced? Tell what happened.

103

"I not only use all the brains I have, but all I can borrow."

— Woodrow Wilson
(28th President of the United States)

All presidents and leaders have advisors. Ordinary people need advisors, too. Whose brains would you most like to borrow, and why?

What are your strongest qualities? How could you use these qualities to advise someone else?

104

"Within the first few months I discovered that being a President is like riding a tiger. A man has to keep riding or be swallowed."

— Harry Truman
(33rd President of the United States)

When you join a club or organization, do you prefer being a leader or a follower? What do you think might "swallow" a president or a vice president?

105

"Politics is war without bloodshed."

— Mao Tse-tung
(Former leader of Communist China)

Think about the fighting between Democrats and Republicans during elections in the United States. What does this quote tell you about the nature of politics in other parts of the world?

106

"Too often we enjoy the comfort of opinion without the discomfort of thought."

— John F. Kennedy
(35th President of the United States)

People form opinions about everything from political candidates to music to whether there's life on Mars. What strong opinions do you hold? How did you form these opinions— through the discomfort of thought or snap judgment?

"And so, my fellow Americans, ask not what your country can do for you—ask what you can do for your country. My fellow citizens of the world: ask not what America will do for you, but what together we can do for the freedom of man."

— John F. Kennedy

Kennedy, the youngest man ever elected to the presidency, was an inspiring speaker. Why do you think the following excerpt from his 1961 inaugural address was so inspirational? What would you ask of your fellow Americans in your first speech as President?

John F. Kennedy

108

"A man does not have to be an angel in order to be a saint."

— Albert Schweitzer
(Alsatian physician, musician, philosopher, and theologian)

Do you think it's possible for any human being to be perfect? Who's the most perfect person you know? List her or his perfect (and imperfect) qualities.

Mini-Bio:
Albert Schweitzer

(Born: January 14, 1875;
Died: September 4, 1965)

When Albert Schweitzer was a boy, he was afraid a friend would make fun of him if he didn't go with the friend to hunt birds. The moment Albert was about to release his slingshot, he heard the bells of a church, and shouted instead for the birds to fly away to safety. This led Schweitzer to his lifelong vow to honor and love all animals and people, which became his famous idea of "Reverence for Life." This philosophy guided him as a doctor, thinker, and musician. Schweitzer started a mission hospital deep within the African jungles and spent a great part of his life helping the people there. Another important idea he held was this: "Wherever a man turns he can find someone who needs him."

109

"Let your conscience be your guide."

— Jiminy Cricket
(Cartoon character in Walt Disney's *Pinocchio*)

"Conscience reigns but it does not govern."

— Paul Valéry
(French poet)

Which of the above quotes do you agree with most, and why? Then select the best answer to the sentence below, and explain your choice.

I listen to my conscience: ___ always ___ sometimes ___ almost never

110

"Whenever there is a crowd there is untruth."

— Sören Kierkegaard
(Danish philosopher)

Can you think of a situation where you went along with the crowd or group against your better judgment? If you could relive that situation, what would you do differently?

111

"Who lies for you will lie against you."

— Bosnian proverb

Have you ever asked someone to lie for you, or been asked by someone to lie? What happened? How did the request affect your relationship with that person?

112

"You cannot make a crab walk straight."

— **Aristophanes**
    (Ancient Greek playwright)

What is this quote saying about human nature? Do you agree? Use an example from your own experience to explain your answer.

113

"What is told in the ear of a man is often heard 100 miles away."

— **Chinese saying**

Do you think it's in human nature to keep secrets? Is it in your nature to keep secrets? Or, is it in your nature to tell secrets to someone else?

114

"A good scare is worth more to a man than good advice."

— **Edgar Watson Howe**
    (American journalist)

Compare a time when you were scared to a time when someone gave you good advice. For instance, have you gone to a scary movie even though people warned you not to go? Based on your experience, what advice would you offer?

115

"I try to learn as much as I can because I know nothing compared to what I need to know."

— **Muhammed Ali**
    (World heavyweight boxing champion)

Muhammed Ali admits that when he was young he thought he knew everything. At this point in your life, how much do you think you know? How much more do you have to learn? Be as specific as you can.

116

"Too much agreement kills a chat."

— **Eldridge Cleaver**
    (African-American author)

How does too much agreement end a chat? Do you think the opposite is true? Can too much argument kill a chat?

117

"God has given you one face, and you make yourself another."

— **William Shakespeare**
    (16th-century English playwright and poet)

Do you think we all change faces occasionally? Do you know anyone who shows one face in school, and another face at home, and still another face with friends? How do you feel when you're around this person?

118

"The darkest hour of any man's life is when he sits down to plan how to get money without earning it."

— Horace Greeley
(American journalist)

Name two ways a person can get money without earning it. Would you recommend either of these methods to anyone you care about?

119

"Before we set our hearts too much upon anything, let us examine how happy they are, who already possess it."

— François de La Rochefoucauld
(17th-century French writer)

Many people would like to be famous and rich. Think of someone who has fame or lots of money, yet doesn't appear to be happy. Consider, too, people who are no longer living. Why do you think this person isn't or wasn't happy?

120

"Rudeness is the weak man's imitation of strength."

— Eric Hoffer
(Longshoreman who became a social philosopher)

Do you agree with Eric Hoffer? Recall a time when you were rude to someone or when someone was rude to you. What do you think prompted the rudeness?

121

"I hear and I forget. I see and I remember. I do and I understand."

— Chinese proverb

"Tell me and I'll forget, show me, and I may not remember. Involve me, and I'll understand."

— Native-American saying

These sayings are from two distinctly different cultures. What do their similarities tell you about human nature? The next time you attempt to learn or teach a skill, such as using a computer program or tying shoes, how could you use the above advice to help you?

122

"No one gossips about other people's secret virtues."

— Bertrand Russell
(English philosopher)

Have you ever heard any gossip that was positive or complimentary? Why do you think people feel the need to gossip? Where do you stand on the issue of gossip?

123

"A book is like a garden carried in the pocket."

— Chinese proverb

What is this proverb saying about the power of a book? Create your own definition of a book by completing the blanks below.

A book is like a (an)

_____.

124

"One could get a first-class education from a shelf of books five feet long."

— Charles William Eliot
(Former President of Harvard University)

What kinds of books would you choose to fill a five-foot-long bookshelf? Think about particular subjects about which you want to learn more such as science or music. Then decide which areas in those subjects you'd like to explore. In science, for example, you may want to study alligators and the aerodynamics of kites.

125

"Reading is a creative activity. You have to visualize the characters, you have to hear what their voices sound like."

— Madeleine L'Engle
(Author of A Wrinkle in Time)

Describe a character from a book who seems like a real person to you. What does he or she look and sound like?

126

Dylan Thomas

"My education was the liberty I had to read...all the time...with my eyes hanging out."

— Dylan Thomas
(Welsh poet)

"Education is not the filling of a pail, but the lighting of a fire."

— William Butler Yeats
(Irish poet)

Besides your teachers and your school, from what other people and places do you receive an education? When you think of getting an education, do you picture a pail or a fire?

127

"All good books are alike in that they are truer than if they really happened…you feel that it all happened to you and after which it all belongs to you."

— Ernest Hemingway
(American novelist)

What's the best book you've ever read? Use Hemingway's idea to review the book. Tell how the book seemed truer than real life, how you felt while reading it, and how the book has stayed with you.

128

"The more I read, the more reasons I found to be proud of my African ancestors."

— John Steptoe
(Author of *Mufaro's Beautiful Daughters*)

What have books or magazines taught you about your own heritage? (Perhaps you've read about a family's journey to Ellis Island, African kingdoms, or Chinese and Irish workers on the transcontinental railroad.) What were the books or magazines? Share two things you learned.

129

"As a Puerto Rican child growing up in New York City, I felt invisible."

— Nicholasa Mohr
(Author of *Nilda*)

When have you felt invisible? If you were a character in a book or a story, how would you describe that feeling?

Mini-Bio: Mark Twain

(Born: November 30, 1835; Died: April 20, 1910)

Samuel Langhorne Clemens was born the night of Halley's Comet, which appears every 75 years. The author of *The Adventures of Tom Sawyer* and *The Adventures of Huckleberry Finn* grew up with an older sister, a younger brother, and 19 cats. Sam was 11 years old when his father died. He had to quit school and work for a printer to support his family (and eventually worked his own way through college!). Always noted for his sense of humor, Sam loved jokes and pranks throughout his life. At the age of 21, he became a riverboat pilot on the Mississippi River, which he loved. There Sam got the idea for his pen name "Mark Twain"—a name used by river men to mean "safe water" (12 feet deep). His restless curiosity led him also to prospect for gold, and become a frontier reporter, humorist, and lecturer. It seems fitting that Mark Twain died at the age of 75, the day after Halley's comet came again.

130

"The man who does not read good books has no advantage over the man who can't read them."

— Mark Twain
(American author and humorist)

How do you feel about reading? Compare the advantages and disadvantages of not reading with those of not being able to read. How do the comparisons affect your views about reading?

131

**"Caesar would have perished from the world of men,
Had not his sword been rescued by his pen."**

> — Henry Vaughan
> (17th-century British poet)

Not only was Julius Caesar one of the great military leaders of all time, but he also wrote about his battles. Caesar died in 44 B.C. What does Vaughan mean when he says that Caesar's sword was rescued by his pen? Think of another person who was "rescued" by someone's pen.

132

"Reading helps you think about things, it helps you imagine what it feels like to be somebody else...even somebody you don't like!"

> — Paula Fox
> (Author of *One-Eyed Cat* and *The Slave Dancer*)

Have you ever identified with a character in a story—felt like that person could be you? Tell about the character. Have you ever really disliked a character? Despite your dislike, did you ever feel what it was like to be him or her?

133

"Reading is to the mind, what exercise is to the body."

> — Joseph Addison
> (English poet and essayist)

How is reading like exercise? What do the two activities have in common? Expand your thinking to make up your own definition for reading.

Tomie de Paola

134

"In celebrating ethnic differences we often discover how much people are really the same. People are people. They all have feelings."

— Tomie de Paola
(Author and illustrator of children's books)

List all the emotions or feelings you can think of that people are capable of expressing. Describe a situation that might cause each one. Do you find that certain situations stir up more than one emotion?

135

"We hate some persons because we do not know them; and will not know them because we hate them."

— Charles Caleb Colton
(English writer)

How would you help a friend or acquaintance overcome their hatred of another person?

136

"Happiness to a dog is what lies on the other side of a door."

— Charleton Ogburn, Jr.
(Author of children's books)

Change the word "dog" to anything you like, then fill in the blanks. Be funny if you wish— consider "mosquito" or "little sister" or "dentist."

Happiness to a (an) _____ is

_____.

137

"One kind word can warm three winter months."

— Japanese saying

When's the last time you offered a kind word to someone? When's the last time someone offered a kind word to you? How did you feel in both instances?

138

"He who hates, hates himself."

— South African proverb

Do you agree with the proverb? Do you know someone who hates but is happy?

139

"I believe that when children behave badly it's because they're hurting."

— Barthe DeClements
(Author of children's books)

Share an instance when you or one of your friends behaved badly because of feeling hurt. Now substitute the word "people" for children. Do you think adults behave badly for the same reasons?

140

"Words once spoken, can never be recalled."

— Wentworth Dillon
(English author)

Have you ever said something in anger that you wish you hadn't said? If the person you spoke against were standing in front of you now, what would you say to him or her?

141

"I was angry with my friend:
I told my wrath, my wrath did end.
I was angry with my foe:
I told it not, my wrath did grow."

— William Blake
(English poet)

Recall a time when you were angry with a friend but didn't tell him or her. What happened? Are you still friends?

142

"The teeth are smiling, but is the heart?"

— African proverb

Have you ever found yourself smiling to cover up feeling sad or embarrassed? Did smiling make you feel better? Tell what happened.

Mini-Bio: Mother Teresa
(Born: August 27, 1910)

Mother Teresa began life as Agnes Gonxa Bojaxhiu, in Skopje, Yugoslavia. She left home at 18 to join the Loreto nuns in India, where she became a teacher and later a principal. When Mother Teresa saw the horrible conditions of the abandoned, starving people on the streets of Calcutta, she left the school and went to Paris to learn medicine. Upon returning, she founded a school for destitute children. Mother Teresa's great love and example have inspired people from all over the world to come to India and join the Missionaries of Charity, her foundation which cares for the poor, ill, homeless, and starving. No one is turned away. She has established many schools and hospitals throughout India, and in 1979 was awarded the Nobel Prize for Peace.

143

"Loneliness and the feeling of being unwanted is the most terrible poverty."

— Mother Teresa
(Humanitarian and winner of the Nobel Prize for Peace)

Do you agree with Mother Teresa? Why or why not? Explain whether or not you think a person can be rich, yet still be poor.

144

"Courage is doing what you're afraid to do. There can be no courage unless you're scared."

— Eddie Rickenbacker
(Fighter pilot)

"Courage is resistance to fear, mastery of fear, not absence of fear."

— Mark Twain
(American author and humorist)

Think carefully about each quotation. Do you agree that fear is a necessary part of courage? Explain your answer.

Mark Twain

145

"I just wanted to make a difference, however small, in the world."

— Arthur Ashe
(Professional tennis player, activist, and humanitarian)

Why do Arthur Ashe's words make him a hero?

146

"When pain ends, gain ends too."

— Robert Browning
(19th-century English poet)

"No gains without pains."

— Adlai Stevenson
(American diplomat)

Since this "no pain-no gain" attitude is usually associated with sports and exercise, what do you think it means when said by a poet? What do you think it means when said by a diplomat who once ran for the presidency?

147

"Delay is preferable to error."

— Thomas Jefferson
(3rd President of the United States)

What does this statement tell you about the way Thomas Jefferson made decisions? Do you think his attitude contributed towards the greatness of the Declaration of Independence (which Jefferson wrote)? Explain why you think so.

Mini-Bio:
Benjamin Franklin
(Born: January 17, 1708; Died April 17, 1790)

Ben Franklin always loved to invent things. Since his home town of Boston was surrounded by water, Ben was always trying to invent better ways to swim: hand paddles, webbed sandals— even tying himself to a kite! His experiments with electricity (and another kite!) led to the invention of the lightning rod. Of course, Ben Franklin was also involved in the creation of the Declaration of Independence and the Constitution. His other accomplishments include running his own newspaper, heading a fire brigade, and founding Philadelphia Academy (University of Pennsylvania).

148

"If you would not be forgotten as soon as you are dead, either write things worth reading or do things worth writing."

— Benjamin Franklin
(American statesman and inventor)

If you could be remembered for one accomplishment after you have died, what would you like it to be?

Will Rogers

149

"Being a hero is about the shortest-lived profession on earth."

— Will Rogers
(American humorist)

Compose a job description that describes the qualifications of a hero. Be sure and spell out the rewards and drawbacks of being a hero.

150

"One machine can do the work of 50 ordinary men. No machine can do the work of one extraordinary man."

— Anonymous

How would you define an extraordinary person? Be sure to include more than one quality that makes someone extraordinary.

151

"I'm just an average citizen. Many black people were arrested for defying the bus laws. They prepared the way."

— Rosa Parks
("Mother" of the civil rights movement)

Tell whether or not you consider Rosa Parks to be "an average citizen." Who appreciates the heroes we never hear about? Can they be heroes if nobody knows about them? Nominate "an average citizen" you know as a hero. What are your reasons for choosing this person?

152

"He could fiddle all the bugs off a sweet-potato vine."

— Stephen Vincent Benét
(American author)

What's heroic about the musician in the above quotation? Name a musician who, in your opinion, is a hero, and reveal what makes her or him a hero.

153

"Greatness is a road leading towards the unknown."

— Charles de Gaulle
(French general and President from 1958-1969)

de Gaulle was a general during World War II. How do you suppose his experiences in battle affected his view of heroes and greatness?

154

"Greatness is a zigzag streak of light-ning in the brain."

— Herbert Asquith
(Prime Minister of England from 1908-1916)

What do you think Mr. Asquith means by this? Can you think of a hero whose brain might work like this? (Think of heros from science, writing, sports, etc.) What makes you think so?

155

"I just wanted to be somebody. I always assumed I would be."

— Natalie Babbitt
(Author of *Tuck Everlasting*)

How can a writer be a hero? Explain your answer. With your answer in mind, name a writer that you might consider a hero.

156

"It is far easier to start something than it is to finish it."

— Amelia Earhart
(First woman aviator to fly the Atlantic solo)

Do these words strike a chord with you, or do you disagree with them? Explain your response. From your own experience, describe a project that was much easier for you to start than to finish.

Mini-Bio:
Amelia Earhart
(Born: July 24, 1898;
Died: 1937?)

As a child, Amelia Earhart hated watching from the sidelines. Once she built a one-car rollercoaster and rode it from her grandmother's shed roof. Earhart also loved the Ferris wheel, and watch-ing daredevil pilots. Finally, after her first ride in an open cockpit plane, she worked to pay for her flying lessons with Neta Snook, the only woman pilot in America at the time. Amelia Earhart started various jobs: nurse's aid to sol-diers after World War I, studying to be a doctor at Columbia University, working as a social worker; but nothing interested her like flying. Even though three women had lost their lives attempting it, she became the first woman to fly across the Atlantic alone. Earhart also flew from Honolulu to the U.S. mainland, and across the country (alone, of course). While attempting a flight around the world, she disappeared. The following quote reveals why she took so many chances in the sky: "Nothing on sea or land can be more lovely than the realm of clouds."

Helen Keller

157

"Science may have found a cure for most evils, but it has found no remedy for the worst of them all—the apathy of human beings."

— Helen Keller
(Humanitarian, author, lecturer, teacher of the blind and deaf)

Helen Keller was blind and deaf from infancy, but never forgot the help she received from her teachers and friends. Subsequently, she spent her whole life helping others. How does knowing this about Helen Keller increase the power of her statement about people who see problems but do nothing?

Have you ever witnessed a situation where someone was in trouble but no one did anything to help? If you could relive that moment, would you try to help? If so, what would you do? If not, why would you ignore the problem?

158

"A sure way for one to lift himself up is by helping to lift someone else."

— Booker T. Washington
(American educator, lecturer, and statesman)

Go over the events of the past week. How did you help "lift someone else"? For instance, did you pick up a piece of paper that someone dropped; did you donate a quarter to a good cause; did you try to cheer up a disappointed friend?

159

"Teach us to give and not to count the cost."

— Ignatius Loyola
(16th-century Spanish founder of the Jesuits)

Does cost always mean money? What's the best gift you've ever received? What's the best gift you've given? How did giving it make you feel?

160

"Worries go down better with soup than without."

— Jewish proverb

Is this proverb saying that when you're worried, you should eat soup? Has anyone ever tried to comfort you? How? What helps to comfort you?

161

"When you cease to make a contribution you begin to die."

— Eleanor Roosevelt
(Former First Lady, reformer, and humanitarian)

We can make many different contributions— to our families and friends, our schools and churches, the environment, and so on. Think of two ways you might make a contribution.

162

"Trouble is a part of your life, and if you don't share it, you don't give the person who loves you a chance to love you enough."

— Dinah Shore
(American singer)

Is there a special person you share your troubles with? Who is it? Does this person share his or her troubles with you?

163

"There is a magnet in your heart that will attract true friends. That magnet is unselfishness, thinking of others first…when you learn to live for others, they will live for you."

— Paramahansa Yogananda
(Spiritual teacher from India)

Who's the most unselfish person you know? Does this person have a lot of friends? What exactly does he or she do (or not do) that attracts friends? List at least two specific things.

164

"He has a heart to criticize, who has a heart to help."

— Abraham Lincoln
(16th President of the United States)

"I don't believe in just ordering people to do things. You have to sort of grab an oar and row with them."

— Harold Geneen
(American businessman)

What do these two quotes have in common? Do you know someone in a position of authority (a boss, a big brother or sister, or a coach) who orders people around but won't assist them? Now think of a person who's the opposite. How do people respond to the two authority figures?

Abraham Lincoln

THE MIND OF THE ARTIST

165

"Every artist was first an amateur."

— Ralph Waldo Emerson
(American poet)

Do you dream of becoming an artist? What kind of guidance do Emerson's words give you?

166

"Drawing is speaking to the eye; talking is painting to the ear."

— Joseph Joubert
(French writer)

Consider carefully what Joseph Joubert said about drawing and painting. What do you think he might say about writing? In addition to the eye or ear, how else might someone respond to writing? Explain your answer.

167

"I dream my painting, and then I paint my dream."

— Vincent van Gogh
(Dutch painter)

Have you ever been inspired by a dream? (Don't forget that inspiration applies to many things: finding an answer to a problem, wanting to learn to sing, or bat better in baseball, getting an idea for a story, and so on.) If you wanted to turn a dream into art, which form would you choose and why? Would you paint it, sing it, write it, mold it, or dance it?

Ludwig van Beethoven

168

"Beethoven can write music, thank God—but he can do nothing else on earth."

— Ludwig van Beethoven
(German composer)

Do you know anyone who's extremely creative in one area, but not in another? Why do you think this is so?

169

"I've been 40 years discovering that the Queen of all colors is black."

— Auguste Renoir
(French painter)

What do you think Renoir meant by the "Queen" of all colors is? What is your "Queen" of all colors? Explain the reasons for your choices.

170

"Music is the shorthand of emotion."

> — Leo Tolstoy
> (Russian novelist)

"Music is your own experience, your thoughts, your wisdom. If you don't live it, it won't come out of your horn."

> — Charlie "Bird" Parker
> (Jazz trumpet player)

"Music is another planet."

> — Alphonse Daudet
> (French novelist)

How does music make you feel when you play or listen to it? Re-read the quotations above, and then create your own definition of music.

171

"Mozart is sunshine."

> — Anton Dvorák
> (Czechoslovakian composer)

Which composer, musician, or musical group "shines" on you? Express your opinion by filling in the blanks below.

_____ is _____.

172

"Painting is just another way of keeping a diary."

> — Pablo Picasso
> (Spanish painter and sculptor)

What do you think Picasso means by this? How would you read a dancer's diary, or a musician's?

173

"In creating, the only hard thing's to begin,
A grass-blade's no easier to make than an oak."

> — James Russell Lowell
> (American poet)

For some people the most difficult part about creating a poem, story, painting, or sculpture—is the beginning. What's the most difficult part of a creative project for you? What do you do to get started? How do you usually feel when you've finished it?

174

"I am sure my music has a taste of codfish in it."

> — Edvard Grieg
> (Norwegian composer)

Edvard Grieg says this because Norway is a country noted for its cod. Think of something you are good at (sports, math, or music) and what might influence it. Complete the sentence below. For example, you might fill in the blanks with "pitching" and "pizza," or "dancing" and "cherry soda."

I am sure my _____ has a taste of _____ in it.

H. G. Wells

175

"Advertising is legalized lying."

— H. G. Wells
(English novelist)

Was H. G. Wells being too hard on advertising? What do you think advertising is?

176

"Television is chewing gum for the eyes."

— Frank Lloyd Wright
(American architect)

What do you think Wright was saying about television? Indicate whether you agree or disagree with the quote by making up your own definition for television.

177

"All television is educational television. The question is: what is it teaching?"

— Nicholas Johnson
(Author of space exploration books)

What do you think Mr. Johnson means by "educational"? Think of at least one thing you've learned from watching television. What was it? How was it presented?

178

"When television is good, nothing is better. But when television is bad, nothing is worse."

— Newton Minow
(Former chairman of the Federal Communications Commission)

Here's your chance to be a television critic! What do you think is the best program you've seen? What's the worst program you've ever seen? Tell why you chose these programs.

179

"Nothing pains some people more than having to think."

— Martin Luther King, Jr.
(Civil rights activist and youngest winner of the Nobel Peace Prize)

Why do you suppose some people are uncomfortable about having to think?

180

"I think and think for months and years. Ninety-nine times, the conclusion is false. The hundredth time I am right."

— Albert Einstein
  (German-born American
  physicist)

What happens when you think and think but reach false conclusions? Do they make you want to quit, or do they encourage you? How do you think wrong answers can help lead you to find the right answer?

181

"How old would you be if you didn't know how old you are?"

— Satchel Paige
  (Baseball pitcher in the Negro
  Leagues, 1927-48, and Major
  Leagues, 1948-65)

If you could choose to be any age right now, which would you choose? Why would you choose this particular age?

182

"A friend is one before whom I may think aloud."

— Ralph Waldo Emerson
  (American poet and essayist)

With which of your friends do you think aloud? How does sharing your thoughts with this friend affect your thinking process?

Mini-Bio: Plato

(Born: 427 B.C.;
Died: 347 B.C.)

Plato's real name was Aristocles, but his gym trainer named him Plato, which means "the broad one." Since he was born of wealthy parents, Plato received a good education in many areas; including sports, poetry, speech, and music. He was a soldier in the Athens cavalry during the Peloponnesian War, which was fought between the city-states of Athens and Sparta. When Sparta won, the Athenians lost many freedoms, including the freedom of speech. Consequently, Plato had to leave Athens for 12 years. Upon returning, he established his own school called the Academy. At the age of 60, Plato was sold into slavery as punishment for his ideas. Friends ransomed him, and he continued to teach his students to always seek the truth, and to endure pain—and even death—for what is right.

183

"When the mind is thinking, it is talking to itself."

— Plato
  (Ancient Greek philosopher)

What does your mind have to say about Plato's words? Do you agree or disagree with him, and why? If the mind talks to itself, do you think it also listens to and argues with itself?

184

"There is no substitute for hard work."

" Genius is one percent inspiration and ninety-nine percent perspiration."

**— Thomas Alva Edison
(American Inventor)**

How are these two statements related? Tell about an accomplishment of your own (a drawing, a project for school, playing in a concert, learning to catch a fly ball, etc.) that was achieved only after lots of "perspiration" on your part.

185

"The game isn't over until it's over."

**— Yogi Berra
(Professional baseball catcher)**

Although Yogi Berra's words seem obvious, consider them from the viewpoint of a player. What kind of inspiration could the quotation give to a player who is behind?

186

"There are people who have money and people who are rich."

**— Coco Chanel
(Clothing designer)**

What do you think Coco Chanel meant by this? Describe someone you know whom you think is "rich" without having a lot of money. Would you rather be rich and unhappy, or poor and happy? Explain your answer.

187

"Everybody is ignorant, only on different subjects."

**— Will Rogers
(American humorist)**

Name one subject about which you know a lot. Now name one subject about which you feel ignorant. Are you interested in losing your ignorance about that subject? If so, how would you go about learning more? If not, explain your lack of interest.

188

"You never know what is enough unless you know what is more than enough."

**— William Blake
(English poet)**

Have you ever experienced what William Blake is talking about? Some examples might be times when you ate too much or stayed out in the sun too long.

189

"Never eat more than you can lift."

**— Miss Piggy
(*Sesame Street* character and puppet)**

Can you see a certain wisdom in Miss Piggy's thinking? Make up your own saying about eating.

Never eat more than you can

_____.

190

"Love, the itch, and a cough cannot be hid."

— **Thomas Fuller**
   (17th-century English clergyman and author)

Give examples of three things that "cannot be hid." Consider feelings as well as objects.

"Why can't somebody give us a list of things that everybody thinks and nobody says, and another list that everybody says and nobody thinks."

— **Oliver Wendell Holmes**
   (American writer)

What would be on your list of things that everybody thinks and nobody says? What would be on your list of things that everybody says and nobody thinks? Compare your lists with other students' lists. How do they differ? After seeing their lists, would you change yours?

Mini-Bio:
Mohandas Gandhi
(Born: October 2, 1869;
Died: January 30, 1948)

Before he became "Mahatma" or "Great Soul" of history, Gandhi was a lawyer in South Africa, who wore fine European suits and had a thriving career. Then he soon began defending the rights of abused Indians in South Africa—often for no money. Gandhi's commitment to injustice was so deep that he returned to his homeland in India. For the rest of his life, he led people in the practice of "satyagraha," or nonviolent resistance. Gandhi owned nothing but homemade clothes, a pair of eyeglasses, and a watch. His patient example changed the course of history and freed his nation of 350 million people from British rule. Gandhi's life ended violently in 1948 when he was killed by an assassin.

191

"To a man with an empty stomach, food is god."

— **Mohandas Gandhi**
   (Spiritual leader from India)

How do you feel when you get hungry? Do thoughts of food block out all other thoughts? If you can't eat right away, how do you try to control your hunger?

192

"You may be disappointed if you fail, but you are doomed if you don't try."

— Beverly Sills
(American opera star)

Which of the following do you believe is best: to succeed every time you try, to try and sometimes fail, or to never try? Use a real-life situation to back up your response.

193

"There can be no real freedom without the freedom to fail."

— Eric Hoffer
(Longshoreman who became a social philosopher)

Do you think anyone could learn to whistle, make a foul shot, or use a computer in just one try? Why is the freedom to fail so important? What's the most important failure you've ever experienced?

194

"Do what you can, with what you have, where you are."

— Theodore Roosevelt
(26th President of the United States)

Theodore Roosevelt took his own advice many times. Think of an emergency situation where his advice might be useful, for example, if you were lost in the woods. How would you use the resources around you?

Wilma Rudolph

195

"I had a series of childhood illnesses. The first was scarlet fever. Then I had pneumonia. Polio followed. I walked with braces until I was at least nine years old."

— Wilma Rudolph
(Olympic track star)

Wilma Rudolph won three gold medals in track at the 1960 Olympics. Do you think her childhood illnesses prepared her for training for and competing in the Olympics? Explain your point of view.

196

"He who laughs, lasts."

— Anonymous

What do you think this quotation means? Apply this advice to overcoming adversity. Choose a time in your own life that you laughed when everything was going wrong. Tell what effect the laughter had on you.

197

"Impossible is a word only to be found in the dictionary of fools."

— Napoleon Bonaparte
  (Emperor of France)

"We will either find a way, or make one."

— Hannibal (247-183 B. C.)
  (Military leader and statesman of Carthage)

Both Hannibal and Napoleon overcame great obstacles to win many military victories. Suppose that Hannibal and Napoleon lived during the same time. What if they had gone to war against each other? Who do you think would have succeeded, and why?

198

"Every path has its puddle."

— Anonymous

What does this saying mean to you? Do you agree with it? Do you feel that one way to overcome adversity is to expect it?

199

"Throughout my career, nervousness and stage-fright have never left me before playing. And each of the thousands of concerts I have played at, I feel as bad as I did the very first time."

— Pablo Casals
  (Spanish cellist and conductor)

Do you ever get stage-fright? How does it make you feel? What do you do to overcome it?

200

"Don't look where you fall, but where you slipped."

— African proverb

Are there other ways of falling besides losing your balance? (Think of unmet homework deadlines, unkept promises, and so on.) Describe one of your falls. What caused you to slip?

201

"Don't look for speed in a cheap horse; be content if it neighs."

— African proverb

Create your own saying based on this proverb. Have fun! For example, you might choose the words "color," "television," and "has a picture."

Don't look for _____ in a cheap _____; be content if it _____.

202

"Those who lose dreaming are lost."

— Australian proverb

Do you know anyone who's given up on his or her dreams for the future? Is this person content? If you could have any dream come true, what would it be?

203

"A chattering bird builds no nest."

— African proverb

"It is easier to talk than hold one's tongue."

— Greek proverb

The proverbs above have a related theme, yet each offers a different insight. What is the related theme? Which proverb says this theme best for you?

Plato

204

"Nothing is so burdensome as a secret."

— French proverb

Give an example of a secret that would be better to reveal than to keep.

205

"Give a man a fish and you feed him for a day. Teach a man to fish and you feed him for a lifetime."

— Chinese proverb

How does this proverb express the difference between giving something to someone and teaching something to someone? Apply its wisdom to a situation in your life—for instance, teaching a little brother to read instead of reading everything to him.

206

"Bad is never good until worse happens."

— Danish proverb

Compare the bad with the worse in the example below:

1. *An ice storm hit your town. (That's bad.)*
2. *Then the pipes in your house froze. (That's worse.)*
3. *Then your furnace broke. (That's even worse.)*

How bad does the ice storm seem now? What lesson does the proverb teach about feeling sorry for yourself?

207

"The price spoils the pleasure."

— French proverb

Apply this proverb to the money value of a product, such as a compact disc or video game. Then use it in connection with something that has no monetary value, such as staying up late to watch a movie and feeling really tired the next morning. At what point does the price become too high?

208

"Better to be quarreling than lonesome."

— Irish proverb

Do you sometimes fight with your brothers or sisters, but really miss them when they're not home? Can you ever be fond of a quarrelsone person?

209

"With money in your pocket, you are wise, and you are handsome, and you sing well too."

— Jewish proverb

If you met someone whom you knew was rich, would you give her or him your honest opinion? Suppose this person made an unwise decision, had on two different colored socks, and sang off key. Would you flatter her or him, or be truthful?

210

"Fall seven times, stand up eight."

— Japanese proverb

Do you share this philosophy? How could you put it to use in your daily life? Give specific examples.

211

"A half truth is a whole lie."

— Jewish proverb

In your opinion, is it ever okay to lie? Back up your opinion with a concrete example.

212

"Don't think there are no crocodiles because the water is calm."

— Malayan proverb

How does this proverb apply to someone who:

1. Sails further than usual in the Atlantic because the sky appears clear;

2. Does not use bug spray on a hike because there are no bugs in view;

3. Skips homework because a substitute teacher is scheduled for tomorrow?

213

"When fire and water are at war it is the fire that loses."

— Spanish proverb

Create your own proverb.

When _____ and _____ are at war it is the _____ that loses.

214

"Listen or thy tongue will keep thee deaf."

— Native-American proverb

Restate the proverb above in your own words. In conversations, which do you prefer doing, talking or listening? If you're a talker, do you sometimes forget to listen, and vice versa?

215

"The man who speaks the truth is always at ease."

— Persian proverb

"If you speak the truth have a foot in the stirrup."

— Turkish proverb

Which of the above sayings about truth do you agree with? Give the reasons for your choice.

INDEX

Angelou, Maya: courtesy of Lordly and Dame, Inc.; Anthony, Susan B.: courtesy of The Library of Congress; Bethune, Mary McLeod: courtesy of The Library of Congress: Chisholm, Shirley: © Moorland-Spingarn Research Center; Clinton, Hillary: © AP/Wide World Photos; Cosby, Bill: © NBC-TV; de Paola, Tomie: Suki Coughlin for Scholastic Inc.; Douglass, Frederick: © The Schlesinger Library, Radcliff College; Earhardt, Amelia; courtesy of The Library of Congress; Ford, Henry: © Ford Archives/ Henry Ford Museum, Dearborn, MI; Frank, Anne: courtesy of Anne Frank Fonds, Basel, Switzerland/Disney; Franklin, Benjamin: © NYPL; Ghandi, Mohandas: © Authenticated News International; Keller, Helen: © The American Foundation for the Blind; Kennedy, John F.: courtesy of The Library of Congress; King, Martin Luther Jr.: United Press International; Lincoln, Abraham: courtesy of The Library of Congress; Mother Teresa: © AP/Wide World Photos; Native American: courtesy of The Library of Congress; Parks, Rosa: © United Press International; Plato: International Portrait Gallery/ Gale Research; Roosevelt, Eleanor: courtesy of The Library of Congress; Roosevelt, Franklin D.: courtesy of The Library of Congress; Rudolph, Wilma: © United Press International; Schweitzer, Albert: © Jerome Hill and Erica Anderson; Shakespeare, William: courtesy of The Museum of Art-Carnegie Institute; Thomas, Dylan: © Marion Morehouse; Truth, Sojourner: © Smith College Collection; Tubman, Harriet: courtesy of The Library of Congress; Twain, Mark: courtesy of The Library of Congress; Washington, George: courtesy of The Library of Congress; Whitman, Walt: © Corbis/Bettmann; Wilson, Woodrow: courtesy of the Bureau of Engraving and Printing; X, Malcolm: courtesy of The Library of Congress.